TALKING THINGS OVER WITH CHEKHOV

by John Ford Noonan

SAMUEL FRENCH, INC.
45 WEST 25TH STREET   NEW YORK 10010
7623 SUNSET BOULEVARD   HOLLYWOOD 90046
LONDON   *TORONTO*

Copyright © 1991 by John Ford Noonan

ALL RIGHTS RESERVED

CAUTION: Professionals and amateurs are hereby warned that TALKING THINGS OVER WITH CHEKHOV is subject to a royalty. It is fully protected under the copyright laws of the United States of America, the British Commonwealth, including Canada, and all other countries of the Copyright Union. All rights, including professional, amateur, motion pictures, recitation, lecturing, public reading, radio broadcasting, television, and the rights of translation into foreign languages are strictly reserved. In its present form the play is dedicated to the reading public only.

The amateur live stage performance rights to TALKING THINGS OVER WITH CHEKHOV are controlled exclusively by Samuel French, Inc., and royalty arrangements and licenses must be secured well in advance of presentation. PLEASE NOTE that amateur royalty fees are set upon application in accordance with your producing circumstances. When applying for a royalty quotation and license please give us the number of performances intended, dates of production, your seating capacity and admission fee. Royalties are payable one week before the opening performance of the play to Samuel French, Inc., at 45 W. 25th Street, New York, NY 10010; or at 7623 Sunset Blvd., Hollywood, CA 90046, or to Samuel French (Canada), Ltd., 80 Richmond Street East, Toronto, Ontario, Canada M5C 1P1.

Royalty of the required amount must be paid whether the play is presented for charity or gain and whether or not admission is charged.

Stock royalty quoted on application to Samuel French, Inc.

For all other rights than those stipulated above, apply to Don Buchwald & Associates, Inc., 10 East 44th Street, New York, NY 10017.

Particular emphasis is laid on the question of amateur or professional readings, permission and terms for which must be secured in writing from Samuel French, Inc.

Copying from this book in whole or in part is strictly forbidden by law, and the right of performance is not transferable.

Whenever the play is produced the following notice must appear on all programs, printing and advertising for the play: "Produced by special arrangement with Samuel French, Inc."

Due authorship credit must be given on all programs, printing and advertising for the play.

ISBN 0 573 69243 2   Printed in U.S.A.

No one shall commit or authorize any act or omission by which the copyright of, or the right to copyright, this play may be impaired.

No one shall make any changes in this play for the purpose of production.

Publication of this play does not imply availability for performance. Both amateurs and professionals considering a production are *strongly* advised in their own interests to apply to Samuel French, Inc., for written permission before starting rehearsals, advertising, or booking a theatre.

No part of this book may be reproduced, stored in a retrieval system, or transmitted in any form, by any means, now known or yet to be invented, including mechanical, electronic, photocopying, recording, videotaping, or otherwise, without the prior written permission of the publisher.

IMPORTANT BILLING AND CREDIT REQUIREMENTS

All producers of TALKING THINGS OVER WITH CHEKHOV *must* give credit to the Author of the Play in all programs distributed in connection with performances of the Play and in all instances in which the title of the Play appears for purposes of advertising, publicizing or otherwise exploiting the Play and/or a production. The name of the Author *must* also appear on a separate line, on which no other name appears, immediately following the title, and *must* appear in size of type not less than fifty percent the size of the title type.

Talking Things Over With Chekhov was presented by Bill Repicci at the Actors' Playhouse under the direction of Marjorie Mahle, with set by Ron Kron, lighting by Tracy Dedrickson, costumes by Gene Lauze, stage management by Joe McGuire, and with the following cast (in order of their appearance):

JEREMY M. .... John Ford Noonan
MARLENE D. ....Diane Salinger

CHARACTERS

JEREMY M.
MARLENE D.

TIME

The present.

PLACE

Riverside Park in the West 80's.

ACT I

Scene 1

SCENE: The time is the present. Autumn, early October. Just after one in the afternoon. The place is a park bench in Riverside Park in the West 80's.

AT RISE: LIGHTS up. Brief seconds and enter JEREMY M. HE is slightly overweight, in very poor condition, and in his early forties. HE sits on park bench. Brief seconds, HE leaps up with renewed verve and looks in both directions. It's as if HE's expecting someone. Suddenly HE spots anticipated visitor, sits back down, and feigns sickness, face in hands, coughing and gagging.

Enter MARLENE D. Tall, beautiful, willowy, late 30's. SHE also wears jogger's suit, along with wool cap and oversized sunglasses. In great shape, SHE stops near bench and does series of advanced stretches. Pleased, SHE sits at opposite end of bench from Jeremy. SHE laughs. JEREMY coughs. Suddenly MARLENE recognizes Jeremy.

MARLENE. Is it you? (*Moves down bench toward Jeremy.*)
JEREMY. Yes?
MARLENE. Marlene?

(JEREMY doesn't recognize her. MARLENE removes a red wool cap from head and sunglasses. JEREMY recognizes her.)

JEREMY. You've ... you've ... you've ...
MARLENE. Made some changes.
JEREMY. Your hair is different.
MARLENE. It's called "The snug look."
JEREMY. You've lost weight.
MARLENE. Almost twenty pounds.
JEREMY. You look taller.

MARLENE. I've reproportioned myself. I work out on a regular basis. Something called the Nautilus machines. I've gotten bigger where I wanted to get bigger. Smaller where I wanted to get small. I feel more held together. People's eyes look at me all different. My body has finally become my friend.

JEREMY. How many times a week?

MARLENE. Three. Plus the running. That I do every day. I start out on the East Side. Cross the Park—rest here for about five minutes. Then the same thing back home. All together it's six-point-two miles. I would die without my six-point-two miles every day.

JEREMY. I've been jogging myself.

MARLENE. It takes a while before the results show.

JEREMY. I just started.

MARLENE. Still got that gut? (*Pats Jeremy's stomach.*)

JEREMY. Please don't touch me like that.

(*SHE doesn't stop. She continues.*)

JEREMY. I hate when you touch me like that I've always hated when you touch me like that.

(*Continues. HER touching grows to tickling. His laughing starts.*)

JEREMY. My stomach's my vulnerable spot. You always do it to get to me.

MARLENE. What's wrong with trying to get to you? (*Tickling increases, laughing grows uncontrollable.*) Am I getting to you?!

JEREMY. Get your fucking hands off my goddamn stomach! (*Suddenly pushes her hands away, leaps up from bench. Quickly HE sits back down, breathing deeply.*) Almost three years and it's like we never—

MARLENE. Two years, nine months, seventeen days.

JEREMY. You keep count?

MARLENE. It's the best way to remember how bad it was.

JEREMY. Marlene, don't start!

MARLENE. I get up in the morning. You're not next to me. I have a reason to live.

JEREMY. Marlene, I'm warning you!!

MARLENE. I look for you every day in the obituaries. I keep hoping you'll get hit by a car. I dream of your funeral. I see the worms getting through.

JEREMY. (*Leaping to feet.*) I don't need this.

MARLENE. No one asked you to sit down.

JEREMY. See you in another three years.

MARLENE. Two years, nine months, seventeen days.

JEREMY. (*Starts off, stops, sits back down on bench.*) So you live on the East Side?

MARLENE. Seventy-third between Park and Lex.

JEREMY. Isn't that expensive?

MARLENE. Herbert makes a ton of money.

JEREMY. When we split up, you swore you'd never live with another man.

MARLENE. We never yell. We never scream.

JEREMY. Sounds pretty quiet.

MARLENE. We're planning to be married in May. I'm meeting his parents this weekend.

JEREMY. Looking forward to it?
MARLENE. Scared to death.
JEREMY. Why do it?
MARLENE. It's important to Herbert.
JEREMY. What about you?
MARLENE. We have a life based on mutual sharing.
JEREMY. It's obviously working. You've never looked better.
MARLENE. When we first get up, he gives me a hug and says, "Hi, BEAUTIFUL, HERE'S ANOTHER DAY." For Herbert it's not a line. It's what he really feels. Herbert's full of feeling. He calls me from work every day around two, no matter what.
JEREMY. Suppose you feel like going out?
MARLENE. He brings me flowers. He surprises me with presents. He's always leaving me notes under my pillow. He calls when he's going to be late. No matter what, we're together every weekend. He remembers the little things.
JEREMY. They all sound pretty big to me.
MARLENE. That's what he's always saying: "ONLY IF BOTH PARTIES REMEMBER THE LITTLE THINGS CAN LOVE GET BIG." He's everything I've always wanted.
JEREMY. Everything I could never be.
MARLENE. He never leaves his clothes around. He never farts ... at least not in front of me. He never picks between his toes and smells it. He never sits playing with his balls. He doesn't need girlie magazines. He's beyond talking dirty. There's nothing with batteries in his drawer.
JEREMY. That was only toward the end.
MARLENE. He does the dishes. Shares the shopping. Oh sweet Jesus, can you hear it in my voice?!
JEREMY. What?

MARLENE. I'm as angry at you as the day I threw you out.

JEREMY. Is that how you remember it?

MARLENE. Don't start with changing things. You're a real ace at clouding everything up.

JEREMY. Next you're going to tell me we were never happy!

MARLENE. For about an hour.

JEREMY. What about the month on Martha's Vineyard?

MARLENE. It was only ten days.

JEREMY. Tell me the three months in L.A. weren't fun?

MARLENE. All I did was vomit and cry. Vomit and cry.

JEREMY. I dare you to tell me the trip to Florida was—

MARLENE. I've got to get out! (*Jumping up from bench.*) If I don't, I'll have nothing right!! (*Starts off in full sprint, three strides, suddenly collapses to ground, holding leg in agony.*) Shit! Goddamn Shit!! Piss fuck shit!!! (*Slapping at left leg.*) Cramp. Left leg. Always when I sit too long.

JEREMY. Want me to rub it?

MARLENE. Someone's got to.

(*JEREMY bends over Marlene.*)

MARLENE. O God. The pain.

(*JEREMY starts to rub.*)

MARLENE. Good. More left. Better. Ah!

(*JEREMY following instruction.*)

MARLENE. Dig deeper ... Hard ... All you've got. Hurt me.

(JEREMY continuing.)

MARLENE. Gone. Help me to the bench.

(JEREMY helps MARLENE to feet, leads her to bench, sits down next to her. SILENCE. MARLENE laughs.)

JEREMY. What's so funny?
MARLENE. That's the one thing you could never do back then.
JEREMY. What?
MARLENE. Help me when I was in pain.
JEREMY. A lot of the time you—
MARLENE. If I had menstrual cramps or that time I couldn't stop crying when Elvis died, you would just turn away and change the subject to something pleasant.
JEREMY. I keep looking for your name in the paper.
MARLENE. See, there you go!
JEREMY. Do you think you'll ever act again? People really miss your acting. Everywhere I go, people who remember us as a pair always ask, "How's Marlene? She's the best young actress we ever watched. I wonder why she just walked away? If you ever see her, tell her we'd like her back!" Everything was going so perfectly. You started with the play at Yale. Moved with it to Broadway. You won the Tony.
MARLENE. Jeremy, I never won the Tony.
JEREMY. You deserved it.
MARLENE. Deserving isn't winning.
JEREMY. What happened that summer at Williamstown after all your success? If you'd still been

with me, I would've helped you through. I would never have let you quit. I would've made you push on. The critics were right: You were the best Masha they ever saw in *Three Sisters*.

MARLENE. This is getting so like Chekhov, I can't breathe.

JEREMY. Remember how I used to come by the theatre all the time and watch you do the third act? I must've caught that third act at least fifty times?

MARLENE. Sixty-three.

JEREMY. And that curtain call. People screaming. Leaping to their feet.

MARLENE. I miss all those "bravos." Jeremy, tell me the theatre needs me back.

JEREMY. Marlene, the theatre needs you back.

MARLENE. Again!

JEREMY. The theatre needs you back.

MARLENE. Tell me something else great.

JEREMY. I've just written my first play.

MARLENE. Come again?

JEREMY. I've written a play.

MARLENE. For the stage?

JEREMY. Two acts.

MARLENE. You've never written a *play*.

JEREMY. That's why it's my first.

MARLENE. What about your critic stuff for the *East Village Other*? What about your acting students—the Melvin Method?

JEREMY. Remember how great you were in my Master Class when you—

MARLENE. That review you gave me for *The Stronger* at the Public with Gerry P.? It was almost—embarrassing!

JEREMY. You knocked me out! You were so deep and dark, and yet so light and if Strindberg himself were to come back right now, he'd have no choice but to—

MARLENE. Is it any good?
JEREMY. What?
MARLENE. Your play.
JEREMY. It's going to be produced.
MARLENE. Where?
JEREMY. At a theatre in the West Fifties called APT.
MARLENE. APT?
JEREMY. Actors and Playwrights Theatre. Part of a new play festival. It's called *The Marathon*. It goes day and night for several weeks.
MARLENE. How many characters?
JEREMY. A man and a woman.
MARLENE. Anything in it for me?
JEREMY. Read it and see.
MARLENE. If I like it, I'll do it!
JEREMY. Why don't we go a step at a time? That way there won't be any—
MARLENE. The publicity people'll have a field day. Actress returns to stage in new play penned by former. It sound so ... so ... so—
JEREMY. Chekhovian—I know. If he were still alive, he and I would've been close friends.
MARLENE. Great artists never have close friends.
JEREMY. I would've been his first!
MARLENE. First what?
JEREMY. Chekhov's first close friend. A great artist needs one. I see us out in Yalta. He coughs. Makes a joke about the weather. I get up. Get him his tea. I come back. His blanket has slipped off. I put it back on. He says, "Thank you" in English. We talk about Tolstoy. I explain how much I love *Anna Karenina*. Chekhov laughs. I ask him why. He only smiles. I smile back. Now he knows I'm truly interesting. He asks about America. I tell him about Brooklyn. He asks why I came all the way to Yalta. "Someone has to take care of you!" "My wife would," says

Chekhov, "but she's in Moscow rehearsing my new play." He bows his head. I ask what's wrong. He says, "As the end approaches, I cry at the silliest things." I take his hand. He whispers, "Thanks, close friend." Suddenly there is wind. Thunder. Before I can—

MARLENE. Jeremy, you've changed, too. You're creating. Making up stories.

JEREMY. Can I finish now?

MARLENE. What?

JEREMY. Me and Chekhov. I was just about to explain how he and I—

MARLENE. I'm already late.

JEREMY. What for?

MARLENE. Till tomorrow. Same place. Same time. One on the button. That way I'll be back home in plenty of time for Herbert's call at two. (*Kissing Jeremy on the cheek.*) Promise you'll bring them tomorrow!!

JEREMY. What?

MARLENE. Five or six copies of your new play.

JEREMY. Why five or six?

MARLENE. I have a hunch about you. I still hate you more than ever, but you've still got that look in your eye. You may have the talent to write something that could bring me back. (*MARLENE starts off.*) CIAO!

JEREMY. Marlene!

(*MARLENE suddenly stops.*)

JEREMY. Please don't say CIAO. I hate people who say CIAO. That's what we used to say.

MARLENE. I'm not well enough to be followed. Please stop following me! (*Exits running.*)

BLACKOUT

ACT I

Scene 2

Again, the park bench in Riverside Park in the West 80's. The following day. It is forty minutes after one.
LIGHTS up. No sight of Jeremy. He is late. MARLENE is dressed in a beautiful wool outfit. Jewels, makeup, the works. SHE paces. Spitting, snorting, growling. SHE is furious. Brief seconds then JEREMY stumbles on in ratty old raincoat, ratty sneakers, ratty hat. In his arm HE carries package wrapped in string. Breathing heavily, HE takes several seconds to catch breath ...

MARLENE. What happened? You're forty-six minutes late.
JEREMY. I got way behind.
MARLENE. Why didn't you grab a cab?
JEREMY. I had nothing but tokens.
MARLENE. Why are you dressed that way?
JEREMY. I've always dressed this way.
MARLENE. Suppose I had people for you to meet?
JEREMY. Marlene, about these people of yours—
MARLENE. Are you still in love with failure? Do you think being unknown and broke is the great crowning glory? Tell me you're not one of—

(Suddenly JEREMY hurls package on ground.)

MARLENE. What's that?
JEREMY. Copies of my play!

MARLENE. How can you call yourself a serious playwright? Would a serious playwright throw his work on the ground?

JEREMY. Shut up or I'll ... I'll ... I'll—

MARLENE. You'll what?!

JEREMY. Don't you understand? It's over!

MARLENE. We were dead years ago, Buster.

JEREMY. That's not what I'm talking about!

MARLENE. What are you talking about?!

JEREMY. It's cancelled!!

MARLENE. What's cancelled?!!

JEREMY. My play in the new play marathon.

MARLENE. When did you find out?

JEREMY. I went over there on my way here. I was supposed to sign a contract. APT's real big on contracts. I walk into the office. Immediately this big guy with a beret wearing glasses says, "Jeremy, all morning we've been trying to reach you!" "What's wrong?" "Our big funding source hasn't come through. We can only do two productions." "Why aren't I one of the two?" "Choices had to be made." "Political or artistic?" "Don't be a wise guy, Jeremy. You're a great writer, Jeremy. Great writers don't have to be wise-guys." A blonde jumps in, "We love your work. Don't let this stop you." I step back and smile like Duvall. "Gentlemen, Ladies, by dark your theatre's going to be a parking lot."

MARLENE. Why did you threaten them?

JEREMY. Cause they were lying.

MARLENE. Lying how?

JEREMY. About why they dumped me! They dumped me because they're terrified of real sex!!

MARLENE. What's that got to do with your play?

JEREMY. My play has serious and deep sexual overtones.

MARLENE. You wrote a play with sexual overtones?

JEREMY. Other people have.

MARLENE. I know but ... but ... How long is the first scene?

JEREMY. I've never timed it.

MARLENE. Read it to me! I'll stop if it gets too long.

(JEREMY tears string from package, tears package open, takes out copy of his script, lays other copies down on bench.)

JEREMY. Ready?

MARLENE. Set the scene.

JEREMY. What's that mean?

MARLENE. Where are we when the play opens.

JEREMY. Fifth floor walk-up. Two-thirty-eight West Fourth Street.

MARLENE. That was our first apartment.

JEREMY. Dawn. A radio plays. The woman sits alone.

MARLENE. Waiting?

JEREMY. Yes.

MARLENE. The man's late?

JEREMY. Very.

MARLENE. An hour?

JEREMY. Almost five.

MARLENE. What's he been doing?

JEREMY. It's in the dialogue.

MARLENE. What's she been doing?

JEREMY. Man enters, she screams, "IN ANOTHER MINUTE I WAS GOING TO CALL THE COPS."

MARLENE. That's me. At least twenty times I said to you, "IN ANOTHER MINUTE I WAS GOING TO CALL THE COPS."

JEREMY. The man says, "I GOT WAY BEHIND."

MARLENE. "I GOT WAY BEHIND" is so you. That's what you said just before, "I GOT WAY BEHIND." Oh sweet Jesus in Heaven, the bum's written a play about us. Jeremy, you super, clever, bastard you.

JEREMY. Marlene, I'm going to continue now.

MARLENE. If it's about us, I might as well read my own part. You read you. I'll read me.

JEREMY. But—

MARLENE. (*Reading from script.*) IN ANOTHER MINUTE I WAS GOING TO CALL THE COPS.

JEREMY. I GOT WAY BEHIND.

MARLENE. WAY BEHIND? IT'S DAWN. WHERE WERE YOU?

JEREMY. WANDERING. THINKING. CONSIDERING.

MARLENE. WHO WITH?

JEREMY. MYSELF.

MARLENE. WHERE?

JEREMY. HUDSON RIVER. NEAR WHERE WE ALWAYS WALK, DOWN BY WEST STREET.

MARLENE. YOU WERE SUPPOSED TO MEET ME OUTSIDE THE STAGE DOOR AT 11:15.

JEREMY. I WAS THERE. Character takes out piece of paper. (*JEREMY acts out taking out piece of paper.*) I TOOK A LOT OF NOTES IN THE LAST ACT. YOU WERE WAY OFF IN THE GOOD-BY WITH VERSHININ. HERE. (*JEREMY gestures as though handing her a piece of paper.*) Here is where the female tears up the note. Do it.

MARLENE. Do what?

JEREMY. Act like you're tearing up the note.

MARLENE. I work only with real notes.

JEREMY. Then say the line after the note.

MARLENE. TARDY BOYS DON'T TELL BROADWAY STARS HOW TO PLAY THE FINAL SCENES IN CHEKHOV. Jeremy, you're good. You have a serious talent. It's us but it's not us. Your dialogue lives.

JEREMY. Can we get back to the dialogue?
MARLENE. But for a first play you're so—
JEREMY. Marlene, stop or I'll take my play away.
MARLENE. It's your line.
JEREMY. THEY WOULDN'T LET ME IN.
MARLENE. WHO?
JEREMY. THAT WOP AT THE STAGE DOOR. HE SAID HE DIDN'T RECOGNIZE ME.
MARLENE. MAYBE IF YOU DRESS BETTER—
JEREMY. THAT'S WHEN MERLIN ZALINSKY CAME BY. I SAID, "MERLIN, HOW 'BOUT GETTING ME IN?"
MARLENE. WHAT DID HE SAY BACK?
JEREMY. "PLEASE, NOT RIGHT NOW."
MARLENE. DID HE EVEN LOOK UP AT YOU?
JEREMY. NO.
MARLENE. HE HAD ONLY YOUR VOICE. YOU CAN'T EXPECT PEOPLE TO KNOW IT'S YOU IF ALL YOU GIVE THEM IS YOUR VOICE. HE HAD A LOT ON HIS MIND.
JEREMY. I HEARD WHAT HE SAID TO YOU IN THE DRESSING ROOM.
MARLENE. I THOUGHT YOU COULDN'T GET PAST THE DOOR.
JEREMY. I WALKED PAST THE ITALIAN. "IF YOU WANT TO EAT SOFT FOODS FOR A MONTH, STOP ME." AS I WAS ROUNDING THE CORNER TO THE DRESSING ROOM, THAT'S WHEN I HEARD MERLIN SAY IT.
MARLENE. SAY WHAT?
JEREMY. "THE WIMP'S WAITING AT THE DOOR."
MARLENE. AND I SAID BACK?
JEREMY. "LET THE WIMP WAIT."

MARLENE. I ONLY DO THAT TO EXPEDITE THE CONVERSATION.

JEREMY. EXPEDITE!!!

MARLENE. THE PEOPLE AROUND ME ARE ALWAYS PUTTING YOU DOWN. THEY MAKE FUN OF YOUR CLOTHES. HOW YOU TALK SO FAST IT SOUNDS LIKE ANOTHER LANGUAGE. HOW YOU HAVE NO TALENT.

JEREMY BUT—

MARLENE. IF I WERE TO STOP THEM AND TELL THEM HOW WARM AND WONDERFUL YOU ARE, HOW SPECTACULAR YOU ARE IN BED, HOW SUPPORTIVE YOU ARE OF MY CAREER, HOW HELPFUL YOUR NOTES ARE WHEN YOU COME TWO OR THREE TIMES A WEEK TO WATCH THE LAST ACT. Jeremy, this is exactly the sort of thing I've always wanted to say to you. (*Returning the script.*) IF I WERE TO STOP THEM AND TELL THEM HOW WARM AND WONDERFUL YOU ARE, HOW SPECTACULAR YOU ARE IN BED, HOW SUPPORTIVE—

JEREMY. You've already said that speech.

MARLENE. But what a speech! If I can do it right, they'll see my character's good side. They'll titter, they'll gasp, they'll cheer.

JEREMY. Marlene!

MARLENE. It's your line.

JEREMY. It's a stage direction. (*Reading stage direction.*) "Man exits and returns with suitcase."

MARLENE. Oh God, it's my line. (*Returning to script.*) WHAT ARE YOU DOING?

JEREMY. SPLITTING.

MARLENE. (*Reads quickly ahead in scene.*) I KNOW I'M A BITCH, A KILLER, A SHARK. TO ADVANCE MY CAREER I'D DROWN A BABY. (*Closing script.*)

This section needs some rewriting. It's too direct. Too melodramatic. I mean, what has she done that's all that bad that he's got to—

(JEREMY rips script out of Marlene's hand.)

MARLENE. I've been thinking about going back to classes. I'm very happy being a wife, I mean, an about-to-be wife. But sometimes I get this ...this ... (*Suddenly taking Jeremy's hand.*) Last week Herbert and I saw Meryl B. in this new play by David L. and I could have done it better. Not the first act, because, well, she is technically a genius. But in the second act where the soul had to shine through, I would have definitely served the playwright better. (*Pause.*) Also, Williamstown has offered me Masha in *Three Sisters* for the summer which I'd love only ... only after what happened last time— (*Suddenly MARLENE stops and puts face in her hands.*)
JEREMY. Are you crying?
MARLENE. Dust in my eye. The West Side's much dustier than the East Side.

(JEREMY turns ahead in Marlene's script and then hands script back to her.)

JEREMY. Read the good-by speech at the end of the scene.
MARLENE. (*Quickly looking speech over.*) She's trying to get him to stay?
JEREMY. Absolutely.
MARLENE. So far as to beg?
JEREMY. What do the stage directions say?
MARLENE. (*Reading from stage directions.*) "Crawls on knees and begs." (*MARLENE gets to knees and reads speech from script.*) I KNOW THE ACTRESS IN ME

KEEPS GETTING IN THE WAY. WHEN THE ENDING COMES TO *THREE SISTERS* AND I AM SAYING THOSE FINAL LINES "IF WE ONLY KNEW, IF WE ONLY KNEW," I STAND SWAYING IN THE MIDDLE, OLGA ON MY LEFT, IRINA TO THE RIGHT, I FEEL AS IF I AM CARRYING FEELINGS SO LARGE AND POWERFUL THAT I COULD ACTUALLY FLAP MY ARMS AND FLY OUT THE BACK OF THE THEATRE. IN THE DRESSING ROOM I CAN'T COME DOWN. OUTSIDE ON THE WAY TO A BAR I CAN HARDLY FEEL THE GROUND. I MUST BE SURROUNDED BY ADMIRERS ONLY. I WANT ONLY TO BE STROKED. NO NORMAL TALK. NO EVERYDAY OBSERVATIONS. I MUST HEAR ONLY "MARLENE, YOU WERE BRILLIANT," "HOLLYWOOD DOESN'T KNOW WHAT THEY'RE MISSING." "EVEN CHEKHOV HIMSELF WOULD'VE HUGGED YOU." I AM SORRY I CAN NEVER BE THERE FOR YOU AT NIGHT. AFTER CHEKHOV, TO BE WITH YOU IS TO BE HELD DOWN. AFTER CHEKHOV, YOU'RE JUST NOT—(*Letting script fall, screaming out to Jeremy.*) Jeremy, how can someone as crazy as you write something as clear as this?

JEREMY. The scene's not over. Can we go back to where—

MARLENE. I can't wait to start rehearsals!

JEREMY. The play's cancelled. There's no production.

MARLENE. We'll do our own.

JEREMY. What?

MARLENE. Herbert wants me out of the house more. He'll back anything I want to do.

JEREMY. But—

MARLENE. Lots of people want to be involved in my comeback. All we need is someone to play you. Sweet Jesus in Heaven, I wonder if he'd consider it?!

JEREMY. Who?

MARLENE. Then there's the director. There aren't many that I'll work with.

JEREMY. What about—

MARLENE. He stinks!

JEREMY. I didn't even say his name.

MARLENE. Jeremy, listen—

JEREMY. Marlene, enough!

MARLENE. Enough what?

JEREMY. (*Slapping bench.*) Sit, *NOW*.

MARLENE. Suppose I don't—

JEREMY. (*Screaming*) *SIT!!*

MARLENE. (*Sitting next to Jeremy.*) Breathe deep. You forget to breathe deep when you're angry.

JEREMY. (*Even louder scream.*) MY MOTHER'S DEAD! STOP!!! (*Pause.*) I wrote this play because I hated you so much. When we first split up, I dated a lot. Everyone I went out with brought you back. A gesture, a smile, a way of holding a cigarette. I gave up dating. Next, every woman I passed on the street became you. I avoided restaurants. I wouldn't board a bus. More and more I spent my days at home. Every night a different movie. Hours browsing in bookstores. One Thursday late I saw a book about Chekhov with his picture on the cover. I bought it. Took it home. Sat it on the desk. Stared at it. His mouth on the cover spoke, "THE MORE YOU HATE, THE LESS YOU REMEMBER!" I grabbed a piece of blank paper. Wrote down a sentence, "IN ANOTHER MINUTE I WAS GOING TO CALL THE COPS." I went to bed. Couldn't sleep. Jumped up. Wrote the next four lines. Thought I saw Chekhov on the cover smile. Then it hit me. That's what writing's about: the real remembering! By dawn I had the whole first scene copied. I read it. It wasn't great, but I saw what I had done. I had taken the resentments and revenges and hates I held against you and I

TALKING THINGS OVER WITH CHEKHOV 25

had stripped them back. What I had found was sadness and hurt and under that the real you. I had gotten back to what was there when we first met. I had dug up the forgotten you, the Marlene I had cared about and trusted. I think that's a great lesson for both of us, don't you?

MARLENE. What?

JEREMY. THE MORE YOU HATE, THE LESS YOU REMEMBER.

MARLENE. I'm glad you said what you said. Cleared the air. Made me aware. I'm too big to cry. (*Picking up copies of play, MARLENE puts them under your arm.*) I'll read it. It could be awful. It could be great. You're just starting out. I remember how I was when I first started out.

JEREMY. Better get going. Don't want to miss Herbert's call.

MARLENE. Good-by, Playwright! (*MARLENE starts off, stops.*) Already I'm getting better. I didn't say CIAO. (*MARLENE exits running.*)

(*JEREMY sits there*)

BLACKOUT

ACT I

Scene 3

Again, the park bench in Riverside Park in the West 80's. The following day. Just after one in the afternoon.

LIGHTS up. JEREMY sits on bench dressed in a lovely tan three-piece suit and holding half-a-dozen red roses. He also wears bowler hat and leaning at his side, a fancy walking cane. Nervously looking left and right, HE spots someone approaching and dashes off. Brief seconds and enter MARLENE D. Hair dishevelled, worn sweater, old and tattered skirt, SHE sits on bench and hums. JEREMY returns laughing ...

MARLENE. I saw you run off.
JEREMY. I couldn't bear to be the one waiting.
MARLENE. Didn't sleep at all, did you?
JEREMY. What a night!

MARLENE. You were always the same back then. Bouncing around, hands flapping like a chicken with its head half off. Talking, so fast no one could—(*MARLENE bursts out laughing.*) 'Member that Sunday you met my mother for the first time? Talk about manic. Jump up. Sit down. Bathroom in. Bathroom out. (*Suddenly MARLENE starts imitating Jeremy from that day.*)

JEREMY. Thank God for Chekhov. He's the only one who can calm me down. After I left you yesterday, I stopped for one drink each at all these different bars. Only works me up more. Get home at 5, flip on *Six Million Dollar Man*. At 6 I switch to 11 for *The Jeffersons* and *Barney Miller*. At 7 back to 5 for *Mash*. I'm exploding. I throw on my sweats. Seventeen times around the block. Up my five flights three and four steps at a time. I swing open my door. Flop to the floor for a set of push-ups. I notice his foot. Stop. Look up. He's sitting in my favorite rocker. Beautiful white linen suit. Felt hat. Walking cane. In his hand a bottle of something Russian. "Like some kvass?" "What's kvass?" He smiles. Pours me half a glass. He toasts, "To you!" "Why me?" "Tomorrow you'll be hearing what people think of your first play." He continues. This visit he's speaking Russian but somehow I hear it in English. "Plays make your life no longer your own. With stories you write it, mail it, good-by. But plays! Rehearsals. Production meetings. Picking the actors." Suddenly he seems about to go on and on. More kvass. He laughs and says, "I don't mind my characters when they go on and on, but I hate to do it myself. How about more kvass?" Another half glass. Now I'm tipsy too. "Close Friend," he mumbles, "you and I are alike in a very big way. We're afraid to let go. We're both way too serious." I smile. He smiles. Now I know why he keeps coming back. He almost drops the bottle and chuckles, "From a tipsy Russian take some silly advice: "ANY NUMBER OF PEOPLE CAN BE LUCKY ENOUGH TO WRITE ONE GOOD PLAY, BUT ONLY A FEW OF US ARE SMART ENOUGH TO DRESS LIKE WE'RE CAPABLE OF WRITING MANY!" Chekhov laughs. I laugh. No two writers have ever howled louder. He goes on, "It's not only how you dress. It's any little thing that makes business easier. The right pencils. Paper you love to touch. A chair to work in that makes your back never hurt. Your desk in front of a window you love to look out of." He grabs my hand so tight I yelp. "CLOSE FRIEND, CONCENTRATE ON THE LITTLE THINGS. THEY'RE THE ONLY THINGS THAT ADD UP." He gets up, flips open the door with his walking cane, and wobbles off. (*Suddenly turning in place like a male model.*) Do I move like a writer of many great—Marlene, what's that ratty dress?

MARLENE. It's how I see myself in Act II.

JEREMY. What about Act I?!

MARLENE. I love it all. Every comma got to me ... It's ... it's ... I only hope I can!

JEREMY. Can what?

MARLENE. Change as much in life as you've made me change in the play. It brought back all my lies. How pushy I was. How East Side I've become. From your play I finally know how I sound. I mean, I knew that's how I sound but I only hear it when I say your words. We had a reading last night.

JEREMY. You should've asked first.

MARLENE. Actually we had two readings.

JEREMY. I'm the playwright. Nothing can be done with my play without first—

MARLENE. Archer Valentine read you.

JEREMY. He's famous. He can do anything.

MARLENE. I'm not so sure he can do you.

JEREMY. He's good enough.

MARLENE. You weren't even there.

JEREMY. But a name like him could really help get my—

MARLENE. At 8 o'clock we had our easy friends in. The ones who are open. Not critical. Before we got to the end of Act I, I heard sniffles. Act II produces several gasps. People leap out of their chairs at the end. Even Adriana De Stephano is taken!

JEREMY. Who's Adriana De Stephano?

MARLENE. We get the first group out quickly. New bottles of wine. Fresh hors d'oeuvres. Pillows fluffed. Herbert renews his smile. The doors are re-opened.

JEREMY. Doors re-opened? What theatre was this?!

MARLENE. We have a seventy-foot living room. Double French doors. The second crowd files in. Now there's a whole different vibration. Critical. Suspicious. Only death impresses them. They sit down. Archer and I go at it again. You could cut the air. The tension is beyond words. You've never acted, but for an actor to perform, you first need—

JEREMY. Stop! Did they like what they heard? Did my great new play go over well?!!

MARLENE. They went more wild than the first group. The coldest bitch in my crowd, Cocky Mendenhall, screamed "THAT'S ME, THAT'S ME" and burst into deep tears.

JEREMY. Did you tell her?

MARLENE. I let her wail on.

JEREMY. Only you, Marlene, only you.

MARLENE. Several people were still crying when their limousines called. Herbert's psychiatrist smiled for the first time since Herbert left his wife for me. A whole group kept yelling "THE NEW YORK THEATRE STILL HAS HOPE!"

JEREMY. I'm good, sure, but let's not—

MARLENE. After we cleared everyone out, Herbert gave me one of his hugs and said, "TO MOVE IN WITH ME YOU DUMPED A BUDDING GENIUS."

JEREMY. "DUMPED"?

MARLENE. Herbert's so mature. Most men would be jealous. Could you see yourself listening to a play written for me by someone else?

JEREMY. I'm sure Herbert felt pretty threatened.

MARLENE. After we do this play and we're all great successes, you've got to get close to Herbert. He's so much what you ... you ...Want to know how my mother compares you two? Herbert's wise and gentle while you're more—

JEREMY. Could we talk a little more about Archer Valentine?

MARLENE. Herbert thinks we can do a whole lot better.

JEREMY. He's the same about you.

MARLENE. Herbert?

JEREMY. Archer.

MARLENE. He's the same about me *HOW*?!!

JEREMY. I met him on the subway coming here.

MARLENE. Archer?

JEREMY. The guy from APT.

MARLENE. APT?

JEREMY. Actors and Playwrights Theatre. *THE MARATHON*? Remember the guy with the beret wearing glasses who I explained—

MARLENE. What's he got to do with Archer Valentine?!

JEREMY. When the guy in the beret wearing glasses ran into me on the train, he had just left a two-hour meeting with Archer.

MARLENE. What was discussed?

JEREMY. Can't you see what's happening? Haven't you a sense where all this is leading?

MARLENE. Tell me.

JEREMY. This time I'm not falling down that hole!

MARLENE. What's that mean?

JEREMY. No matter what, I cannot be around this.

MARLENE. Be around *WHAT*?

JEREMY. I'm going with someone else.

MARLENE. Someone else *WHERE?*

JEREMY. In your part. Rehearsals start a week from Wednesday.

MARLENE. Is Archer playing you?

JEREMY. Yes.

MARLENE. Who's doing me?

JEREMY. Constance Guthrie.

MARLENE. I've never heard of her.

JEREMY. She's amazing. Fabulous. Wonderful.

MARLENE. What have you seen her do?

JEREMY. Actually—

MARLENE. You've never seen her work, have you?!!

JEREMY. That doesn't mean—

MARLENE. How do you know she can do me?!!

JEREMY. The guy in the beret wearing glasses and Archer both consider her the best available choice. The guy in the beret and I really get along. He's crazy. Mad. Mean.

Vicious. He makes me feel like a brother. When he starts to talk, you know he knows what he's saying. He's had nothing but trouble with actors playing parts in plays written for them by friends.
  MARLENE. But he's never seen me work!
  JEREMY. He finds your technique lacking. He says in emotionally demanding scenes you tend to push.
  MARLENE. What's he seen me in?
  JEREMY. If Constance Guthrie doesn't work out as you, he and Archer both agree you'll be the one to step in next.
  MARLENE. Jeremy, don't do this to me!
  JEREMY. Art's not about old friends. The play's the star. Not you. Not me.
  MARLENE. I'll do anything!
  JEREMY. It's all been done!
  MARLENE. Do you know how hard it is to be me? How can this other woman even start to be me? Do you know what makes me up? Even a brilliant actress would need months and months!

(JEREMY starts to go, MARLENE grabs him by the arm.)

  MARLENE. Let me do the monologue from the end of Act I. I've got it almost all memorized. Tell me "OUT OF THE WAY" and give me a big shove.
  JEREMY. What are you talking about?
  MARLENE. That's how your first act ends.

(Again JEREMY starts to go, again MARLENE grabs him.)

  MARLENE. See, you're so confused you've forgotten how your first act ends!

JEREMY. Tomorrow could we meet? Same time? Same place.

MARLENE. What for?

JEREMY. To get the copies of my play back! Nothing against you but I don't want any loose copies floating around.

(JEREMY starts off, MARLENE dives to tackle him, misses, ends up on ground.)

JEREMY. I'm tired. I'm scared. I'm happy. I'm worried. I'm lonely. I am sorry but I have nothing more left for you today (*JEREMY starts to go, rushes back to Marlene on ground.*) Please be on time with my play. Don't make me send people after you.

(Exit JEREMY in a rush. MARLENE continues to sit on ground.)

BLACKOUT

End of Act I

ACT II

Scene 1

Again the park bench in Riverside Park in the West 80's. The following day. One in the afternoon.

LIGHTS up. MARLENE sits alone on bench. On her lap the five copies of Jeremy's play neatly bound by string. She is wearing a lovely fall outfit. SHE looks beautiful and serene. For a reason known only to her, SHE laughs to herself, can't stop, holds stomach, laughing on ... as JEREMY enters. He is wearing same outfit as yesterday but it looks slept in, haggard...

JEREMY. Is that a new dress?

MARLENE. I always look great when I'm falling apart. I don't know if you remember this, but the first month we lived together my father died.

JEREMY. I wanted to accompany you to the funeral. I remember you screaming back: "FAMILY! STAY OUT!!"

MARLENE. At the cemetery I looked absolutely ravishing. As they lowered his casket into the ground, everyone's eyes were on me. When I told Herbert last night that you were using someone else to play me—

JEREMY. Marlene, listen! I have something to—

MARLENE. He smiled, put his arm around me and sat me down in the couch. We have that couch you and I used to admire from that antique store on Columbus and 87th. Herbert bought it for me for our second anniversary.

JEREMY. Marlene, that's all very nice but—

MARLENE. So we're sitting there, me in tears and Herbert says, "WE ADMIRE JEREMY'S PLAY MORE

THAN EVER. WE STILL LOVE THE CHARACTER HE BASED ON YOU. WE WANT IT TO RUN FOREVER." Suddenly I scream, "SO TELL ME WHAT WE DO?" Herbert smiles and says, "LET'S SIT WITH THE PLAY AND LET IT TELL US." We each lay a copy across our laps. Herbert opens to page one and begins reading me. I do you. We stop after six pages. The doorbell rings. Our two favorite actors from upstairs. They take over. We listen. They read the play through a second time. Suddenly all four of us zero in on Act II. Our two actor friends read through Act II three consecutive times.

JEREMY. They must've really loved my words! Who are they?

MARLENE. They're famous but they're both wrong for the play!

JEREMY. But who's to—

MARLENE. The four of us tear apart Act II for over two hours.

JEREMY. Hold it! Where do you get off—

MARLENE. Herbert brings out his recording equipment. He loves anything mechanical. We each speak what we feel. All four of us agree on two things: Act I is perfect or nearly so; and Act II can be taken a whole further step. (*Handing Jeremy copies of his play neatly wrapped.*) Inside all our suggestions are neatly typed up. That's a good play. It has the potential to be great. Please do the goddamn work!

JEREMY. (*Hurling package of scripts to ground.*) Chekhov told me the same thing. Goddamn pain-in-ass Russian know-it-all. (*Suddenly kicking at package.*) I wanted my first play to be fun. Peaceful. Pleasant. No waves. All smiles. No people around me who make my stomach hurt. Young girls who know nothing about me except that I'm the author of a startling new work!

MARLENE. Jeremy, it can never—

JEREMY. Yesterday I got drunk after I left you.

MARLENE. With me you never overdid anything!

JEREMY. I stumble up the stairs. My door is already open. He's sitting there in his only dark suit.

MARLENE. How do you know it's his only dark suit?

JEREMY. He says, "This is my only dark suit." This time he sounds almost English. I say "Anton, Close Friend, why a new accent every day?" He smiles and says "Today no questions, Fellow Writer. Today you do nothing but hang your arrogant ears on the nail of humble attention." I scream, "no one can call me arro—" Suddenly he grabs my vodka bottle, downs the last swig, and slams me into my chair at my work desk. He grabs my neck and twists it to face the far, bare wall over my bed. With one of my magic marker pencils he has scrawled, "GOOD ART NEVER EXCUSES BAD LIVING." I scream "Sober up and make sense." He slaps my face and says, "I ALSO WANTED IT TO BE FUN. PEACEFUL. PLEASANT. NO WAVES. ALL SMILES." I'm stunned. Finally to meet someone who knows even more than me. He takes my hand and explains, "Close Friend, you can't just write a play. You've got to go through with it. When I finished *Three Sisters*, I wanted to stay in Yalta. A blanket around me, smiling at the sun, waiting for that young girl to bring me the reviews. Close Friend, writing a play is like baking a cake. Every step you skip shows up in the end. I got up my strength, hitched up the horses and started for Moscow. The bumpiest ride of my life. Awful food at every stop. My sister Anna greets me at the door. Olga's out shopping. They cook me a wonderful dinner. Next day rehearsals start. I sit through them all. Every last one. I'm open to rewriting. The speech that ends the play, "IF WE ONLY KNEW, IF WE ONLY KNEW!" —I write the eleventh day of rehearsal. After rehearsals I greet people on the street. I shake hands. I accept admiration. I am shy. I am scared but I am taking every little step to make my cake come out right. Every night before retiring I get on my knees and say, "I MAY DIE OF TB BUT I WILL NOT DIE OF ARROGANCE. I AM FOLLOWING MY LITTLE STEPS. MY LITTLE STEPS ARE ADDING UP." Chekhov is now smiling. My writing friend wears a glow. He takes my hand and says, "Young Fellow, she is your biggest little step of all." For a second, confusion, but then I knew. I smile. Get hold of my glow. (*Suddenly holding Marlene's hand.*)

MARLENE. Why are you holding my hand?

JEREMY. I want you in my play. I won't do it with anyone else.

MARLENE. Again!

JEREMY. I want you in my play. I won't do it with anyone else.

MARLENE. One last time!!

JEREMY. I want you in my play. I won't do it with anyone else.

MARLENE. Say, "MARLENE, I'LL KILL MYSELF IF YOU'RE NOT UP ON THAT STAGE OPENING NIGHT."

JEREMY. I'LL KILL MYSELF IF YOU'RE NOT UP ON THAT STAGE OPENING NIGHT!

MARLENE. Say, "BROADWAY HASN'T GLOWED SINCE YOU HAD YOUR BREAKDOWN."

JEREMY. BROADWAY HASN'T GLOWED SINCE YOU HAD YOUR BREAKDOWN!

MARLENE. Say, "MARLENE, YOU'RE THE GREATEST ACTRESS OF OUR TIME. IT MUST BE SOMETHING VERY SICK IN ME THAT MAKES ME PUNISH YOU FOR YOUR TALENT."

JEREMY. MARLENE, YOU'RE THE GREATEST ACTRESS OF OUR TIME. IT MUST BE SOMETHING VERY SICK IN ME THAT MAKES ME ... MAKES ME

TALKING THINGS OVER WITH CHEKHOV   37

... (*Suddenly stops, lets out a muffled cry.*) Since I ran into you a few days ago, I've gotten all whipped up. Filled with these ... these ... They've all come rushing back. I can't eat! I can't think!!

MARLENE. Stomach's in a knot. Brain on fire.

JEREMY. Exactly! And I go to bed ... only an hour later I wake up screaming for you

MARLENE. "MARLENE., HOLD ME, SAVE ME, MAKE ME WHOLE!"

JEREMY. Exactly! This morning I tore up the closet for that old picture of you!

MARLENE. In my bathing suit from that last happy summer in Williamstown?

JEREMY. Exactly! I'm a wreck. I don't want to ...to ... (*Suddenly beats at stomach with furious fists.*) I'm so scared! So scared!! So scared!!! Thank God for you and Chekhov. I can't wait for rehearsals.

MARLENE. First, I'll have to see the second act rewrites.

JEREMY. Please don't!

MARLENE. Can you see them?

JEREMY. WHO?!!

MARLENE. The opening night audience. (*MARLENE "acts out."*) Curtain up. Me and the guy playing you charge out of the gate. No more than ten minutes and we've got them riveted. They gasp at the first act ending. The lobby's buzzing. Hear the buzz? Catch the chatter? (*Suddenly "imitating WOMAN" in lobby.*) "O GOD, IRENE. THE MALE CHARACTER'S JUST LIKE MY FRED!" Look over in the corner. Two gays giggling. (*Acts out "Two gays giggling."*) And that eighty-two-year-old blue-haired lady in mink whispering to the boy working the concession stand. (*Suddenly imitates "eighty-two-year-old lady."*) "... HAD I DIED LAST YEAR, I WOULD'VE MISSED THIS!" Your first act has unified the crowd. Now they're filing back in for the second act. They're expecting the birth of a true, honest-to-goodness original. They all want to be able to say, "YES, I WAS THERE THAT INCREDIBLE NIGHT." Jeremy, the second act as written now and they'll get angry. Mad. You promised roses and delivered dandelions.

JEREMY. Yesterday you said it was the greatest thing since—

MARLENE. And the critics! The one, clear, unmistakable thing that unifies them is disappointment. Once a year on Broadway they let their anger out, not at some amateur American or overrated Britisher, but at some promising talent who pumps them up in Act I and doesn't deliver in II. Please don't let them hang you by the ankles. Please don't let them make you never want to write again.

JEREMY. Tell me where to start.

MARLENE. The SEX!!

JEREMY. WHAT?!!

MARLENE. All this moaning and groaning and who screamed the loudest.

JEREMY. We were an exceptionally loud pair!

MARLENE. What about those final months when the only conversations were notes scribbled to each other on the bathroom mirror?

JEREMY. Hold it! I thought —

MARLENE. What were we both afraid of? Why was it a look of need in your eyes and I'd disappear for days?!

JEREMY. But —

MARLENE. At the end we were even too tired to scream. (*Suddenly grabs Jeremy.*) Hate like ours is special. Dig down. Look around. Forget your glands. Talk from the heart. Bad art's about what we already know. Good art's about where we've never been.

JEREMY. (*Writing in "pocket notebook."*) "Bad art's about what we already know. Good art's about where we've never been."

MARLENE. It's the last thing Herbert says ever night when we're going to bed.

JEREMY. Is there anything Herbert doesn't do?

MARLENE One thing he won't do is produce the play with Archer Valentine.

JEREMY. I already promised it to him.

MARLENE. Right now Herbert's explaining to him why he's not good enough. We need a secure star or a brilliant unknown. Someone dangerous, brilliant, moody, incredible. Casting people all over town are already hot on it. You of course will have final approval.

JEREMY. Anything else you want to let me in on?

MARLENE. During rehearsals only the director gives me notes. I'll listen to anything you have to say but only and always through him.

JEREMY. What's his name?

MARLENE. Howard Macklin.

JEREMY. He's the best. Where'd he come from?

MARLENE Herbert locked him up this morning.

JEREMY. You knew all along, didn't you?

MARLENE. (*Suddenly laughing.*) Wouldn't it be something if this were only the beginning.

JEREMY. Beginning of what?

MARLENE. One play isn't enough. You write another—call it HOW THE FIRST WASN'T ENOUGH. Go on to a third. That one's titled ONLY A THIRD WILL DO. Play after play your main character is always me. Every time I'm the perfect one to play it. We grow together. We're always mentioned in the same breath. We're a leading artistic tandem.

JEREMY. What about our personal lives? What about these feelings I have for you that won't—

MARLENE. Put it into the rewrites!

JEREMY. Give me some hope for us. A word, a gesture, your old smile, what about —

MARLENE. (*Smiling*.) The rewrites are due a week from today. Same time. Same place. I'll be here.

JEREMY. But —

MARLENE. None of your Catholic long-hand. (*Reaching into pocket, business card, handing to Jeremy*.) Here's her number. A hundred words per. Any time of the day or the night she can be at your door in twenty minutes.

JEREMY. Marlene, I can't afford to pay a woman to —

MARLENE. (*Reaches into pocket, hands Jeremy green savings passbook*.) Herbert opened an account at the bank on your corner in the Village.

JEREMY. (*Reading from savings book*.) Five Thousand?

MARLENE. Consider it your option money.

JEREMY. The guy in the beret wearing glasses told me that the standard first payment was only—

MARLENE. (*Handing Jeremy second card*.) Call your new agent. Let him fill you in.

JEREMY. But—

MARLENE. (*Handing Jeremy third card*.) If you have trouble sleeping, here's a doctor. (*Handing Jeremy fourth card*.) If you need to stay awake, here's another. (*MARLENE suddenly puts hands around Jeremy's neck and gives him long, sustained "soul kiss."*) Work hard, Gifted Playwright!

(*MARLENE runs off. JEREMY sits on bench. JEREMY holds script.*)

BLACKOUT

ACT II

Scene 2

Again, the park bench in Riverside Park in the West 80's. Two weeks and two days later. Twenty minutes after one.

LIGHTS up! MARLENE sits alone on bench. Sweat suit, running sneakers, Does series of stretch exercises, checks watch, does series of deep breathing to relax. Lets out eight or nine horrendous screams of rage. Enter JEREMY. HE is tired, drawn, red-eyed, clothes dirty, bloody, wobbly with exhaustion. He wears an enormous raincoat. Over his eye a butterfly bandage to cover cut requiring ten stitches ...

JEREMY. Sorry I'm late.

MARLENE. It's only nine days.

JEREMY. Each day when I knew it was another day, one o'clock made me feel something very ... very ... Twice I threw up. Once I cried. Today when I saw I was going to finally get here, God, did I want to be on time. I tried my best. Twenty minutes is a lot better than the old days.

MARLENE. The other night at a party given by the mayor to raise money for the New York City Ballet, I met a man named Eddy October who, when he heard what you had pulled, smiled and said, "LET'S HAVE THE FUNERAL ON A TUESDAY. THREE THOUSAND TWO HUNDRED FIFTY-FIVE IN CASH IS ALL IT TAKES!"

JEREMY. Why three thousand, two hundred fifty-five?

MARLENE. (*Exploding.*) You don't deserve to live, you worm, you inanimate piece of ... of ... Generous, kind, and caring people count on you and you just ...just ...

JEREMY. I'm beat. Burned. It's been a rough coupla weeks. Why don't we just—

MARLENE. The detective reported everything! (*MARLENE produces two pages of Jeremy's activities. Reads slowly, a bomb ready to go off.*) The first night you got into a fight outside *Page Six,* a Village after-hours club. 6:18 A.M. Cocaine dripped from your nose.

JEREMY. Want to hear what started it? I told this producer guy about the play. He says "SHE'S THE MOST OVERRATED TALENT IN THE AMERICAN THEATRE!"

MARLENE. The third day you took thirty-seven hundred out of your account.

JEREMY. What's this? Russia!

MARLENE. Tell me about the five hookers at the start of the second week?

JEREMY. I figured reading them the first act might —

MARLENE. Tell me about the cocaine.

JEREMY. I did a lot.

MARLENE. How much heroin?

JEREMY. Once scared me.

MARLENE. The report says *three* times.

JEREMY. O.K., three times scared me more.

MARLENE. Is it or is it not true that the night before last you offered one Julio Mendez two hundred dollars to shoot you?

JEREMY. Since I couldn't do the rewrites, I figured—

MARLENE. Did you or did you not spit in a policeman's face and then when he pulls his gun, you laugh and say, "I'LL CATCH THE BULLET AND STICK IT RIGHT BACK UP YOUR ASS!" Night before last did you actually—

JEREMY. Did your detective tell you what I did to Chekhov?!

MARLENE. Tell me!

JEREMY. I threw him down the stairs.

MARLENE. *WHAT*?!!

JEREMY. I crawl up the stairs. Door open. He's nowhere to be seen. Suddenly I hear the toilet flush. The door opens. He's got on the smoking jacket Gorky gave him. He's wearing a smile I've never seen before. Already I'm pissed. "Writing Friend," he says, "we'll need more toilet paper soon!" I want to rip out his throat. Next he directs me to the far wall. Where earlier he had scrawled, "GOOD ART NEVER EXCUSES BAD LIVING," now he's written, "LET ANTON CHEKHOV BE FOR YOU WHAT LEO TOLSTOY COULDN'T BE FOR HIM." He puts his arm around my shoulder. "Talented Friend," he says with just the trace of a French accent, "not only is dear Marlene right about the sex in Act II, but these two people can't end up together in the final scene." "Russian Schmuck," I scream, "it's why I'm doing it. To end up with her in the end!"

MARLENE. Jeremy, listen: if that's—

JEREMY. Suddenly Chekhov pulls out a copy of *Cherry Orchard*. "I had the same problem as you writing my final act. I wanted so badly for things to turn out happy. I was so desperate for Lopahin and Varya to end up together that I pulled my own ten-day vodka bender." Through his tears he talks on. "Like you, all I needed was someone looking over my shoulder. I went to Tolstoy. Much as the bouncing carriage hurts, I make his house in less than a day. I knock ... The minute I see the white beard, I say, "Uncle T, I am having trouble finishing the last act of my new play. Will you come and cast a warm shadow?" He laughs that laugh of his. "Anton, your fiction is superb, but as I told you at the opening of *Three Sisters*, that snowy night in St. Petersburg, I hate your plays." "Uncle T, you were drunk." "I will tell you the same thing sober. YOU ARE WORSE THAN SHAKESPEARE, do you hear me, WORSE THAN SHAKESPEARE!" He slams the door. I begin to laugh. I crack the reigns. The sled starts for home. I keep laughing and yelling proudly at the snowy countryside, "WORSE THAN SHAKESPEARE! WORSE THAN SHAKESPEARE." Marlene, I have never seen him so happy as he was in telling this story. That's when he turns to me, his smile fading as quickly as it had come. His hand lies heavy on my arm, the tears are filling up again, and in a choking, quavering whisper he says, "I had to let my characters not end up together, and you must do the same." That's when I pick him up and throw him down the stairs.

MARLENE. It wasn't you, Jer. It was all the cocaine.

JEREMY. The sound of him tumbling was awful. He yells back: "IT'S A COMPOUND. I'LL HAVE THEM SET IT AT ST. VINCENT'S. READ THE WALL TILL I GET BACK."

(Long SILENCE. JEREMY stands relaxed, smiling broadly. MARLENE, nervous, ready to leap.)

MARLENE. Did he ever get back? Is he alive? Dead? WHAT?!!
JEREMY. Ready to read my new second act?

(MARLENE cannot form the words. SHE is so stunned. Out of his left pocket HE pulls copy of new Act II.)

JEREMY. Finished it an hour ago. (*Out of left pocket HE pulls second copy. Crosses to her, hands it to her.*) Marlene, a Xerox for you. That's why I was late. Old machine. Didn't collate. Me and some Chinese kid all by hand.

MARLENE. Jeremy, if you think you're going to pass off something you whipped off during some drug-induced—

JEREMY. You've got the opening lines.

MARLENE. (*Reading from script.*) I PACKED YOUR BAGS. I KNOW IT'S TIME AGAIN.

JEREMY. I NEVER GOT TO SEE ANY OF IT.

MARLENE. SEE ANY OF WHAT?

JEREMY. FIRST ROW OF THE BALCONY. NEXT TO ME, TWO GUYS ABOUT THIRTY. THE LIGHTS GO OUT. THE CREDITS ROLL. CAMERA JAMS. FILM GOES CRAZY. LIGHTS FLASH BACK ON. CROWD BELOW IN THE LODGE GOING WACKY, THROWING ALL KINDS OF CRAP AT THE SCREEN. THE GUY AWAY FROM ME SAYS TO THE GUY NEXT TO ME, "WATCH MY POPCORN. I WANNA CATCH HER BEFORE REHEARSALS."

MARLENE. Jeremy, this is hardly the sort of thing I—

JEREMY. THE ONE LEFT NEXT TO ME OFFERS ME POPCORN. I SMILE. THE OTHER RETURNS. "MISSED HER. HER MACHINE SAYS AFTER ELEVEN SHE'LL BE AT THE CAFE." THE GUY NEXT TO ME LAUGHS, "AREN'T YOU EVER AFRAID OF HER OLD MAN CATCHING ON?"

MARLENE. Jeremy, really now. Broadway won't —

JEREMY. CATCHING ON TO WHAT? HE'S A WIMP!! TO THE GUY WHO OFFERED POPCORN I WHISPER, "I'M THE WIMP. WANNA WATCH?" IN TERROR HE FLIES UP THE AISLE. NOW IT'S JUST ME AND LOVER BOY. (*Suddenly JEREMY leaps to feet and begins "ACTING OUT" incident.*) I WHIP OUT MY NEW SCHAEFFER INK PEN AND STAB HIM IN THE CHEEK. "INK AND BLOOD," I SCREAM. "INK AND BLOOD." HE TRIES TO RUN. I SLASH AT HIS EAR.

A PIECE COMES OFF ON THE TIP OF MY PEN. HE SCREAMS, "POLICE! POLICE!!" BUT I STUFF THE POPCORN BOX IN HIS MOUTH AND GO FOR HIS THROAT. I SPIT, "WHAT'S IT LIKE INSIDE HER? SHE EVER SCREAM OUT MY NAME?" I THROW HIM OVER THE RAILING AND GRAB HIS ANKLES. I SCREAM, "SAY YOU'LL NEVER SEE HER AGAIN." "UP YOURS, WIMP!" I DROP HIM. A SPLIT SECOND AND THEN ON THE CEMENT.

MARLENE. O GOD, DID HE LIVE?
JEREMY. DID *WHO* LIVE?!
MARLENE. FRANK! IS FRANK LIVING?!!
JEREMY. WHAT'S HIS NUMBER?!
MARLENE. 838-1165.

(Suddenly from out of pocket of raincoat JEREMY pulls cordless phone receiver with push buttons in handle. Quickly dials number, hands phone to Marlene.)

JEREMY. Ask Frank yourself!

MARLENE. (*Taking receiver.*) GOD, I'LL DIE IF HE—(*Suddenly stopping.*) HOLD IT! HOW CAN HE BE ALREADY HOME IF YOU JUST— (*Bursting into laughter, MARLENE hugs Jeremy.*) Jeremy, brilliant, brilliant, brilliant. You tricked me, I mean, my character into—

JEREMY. (*Pulling back.*) Please stick to the script.

MARLENE. It's your line!

JEREMY. (*Pantomimes handing note to Marlene.*) READ SLOW! HIT THE WORDS HARD UNDERLINED IN RED!

MARLENE. (*Into receiver.*) FRANK, GOOD-BYE. DON'T CALL. THANKS FOR NOTHING.

JEREMY. NEXT WE CALL MARK T. AFTER THAT ROBBY C. THERE ARE ONLY THREE, RIGHT?

MARLENE. For so long Broadway has wanted to see me in something like this. Dangerous, dark and yet —

JEREMY. Marlene, just say the next line. Forget —

MARLENE. The scene has real drive. True momentum. Herbert believed in you. I doubted. We've got him to thank.

JEREMY. (*Angrily turns pages of Marlene's script forward.*) Try near the end! (*Stabbing gesture points toward something on new page.*) Say it!

MARLENE. What a breakdown speech. Guts all over the floor. Once I'm able to personalize the feelings, I'll have the audience eating out —

JEREMY. I want my words, *NOW*!

MARLENE. Go back a few lines. Warm me into it. Break me down!

(*JEREMY turns to previous page in revised Act II. Just as JEREMY is about to start, MARLENE makes suggestion*)

MARLENE. Start with "FRANK IS NOT THE FIRST TIME."

JEREMY. (*From script.*) FRANK IS NOT THE FIRST TIME. I FOLLOWED YOU TO THE MAYFLOWER OVER A YEAR AGO. I STOOD WITH MY EAR TO THE DOOR. I HEARD THE SCREAMS THAT SHORT ACTOR GOT OUT OF YOU.

MARLENE. Jeremy, listen —

JEREMY. The character's called "MARVIN."

MARLENE. MARVIN, LISTEN—

JEREMY. I KNOW ABOUT THE GUY IN THE MOTEL AFTER YOUR FATHER'S FUNERAL. I KNOW ABOUT THE DIRECTOR BOTH ON BROADWAY AND UP IN WILLIAMSTOWN. I KNOW

ABOUT THE ACTOR WHO UNDERSTUDIED SOLYONY!

MARLENE. I REALLY DON'T COUNT ONE TIME AS—

JEREMY. ALL I WANT TO KNOW NOW IS: ARE THERE ANY I MISSED? IS IT O.K. TO GO TO THE MOVIES AND NOT EXPECT ANOTHER FRANK? (*MARLENE stands there. LONG SILENCE. No reaction. JEREMY in a stage whisper.*) The script says "SMILE"

MARLENE. I'm a slow smiler. (*MARLENE slowly finds a smile*).

JEREMY. WHY ARE YOU SMILING THAT SMILE? THAT'S NOT A SMILE I KNOW.

MARLENE. REMEMBERING.

JEREMY. REMEMBERING?

MARLENE. THE EXCITEMENT.

JEREMY. WHAT OF?

MARLENE. KNOWING YOU KNEW.

JEREMY. YOU KNEW I KNEW?

MARLENE. I FELT YOU OUTSIDE THE DOOR AT THE MAYFLOWER. IT ADDED TO MY SCREAMING. EVERY TIME I LEFT THE HOUSE TO GO GET IT, I FELT YOUR EYES FOLLOWING.

JEREMY. WHY DID YOU NEVER SAY TO ME, "I KNOW YOU KNOW? FEELING YOUR EYES FOLLOWING IS BREAKING MY HEART"?

MARLENE. BREAKING MY HEART?!! (*Laughing.*) I WAS HOT ALL THE TIME. YOUR EYES BEHIND, HIS COCK AHEAD. I WAS QUEEN. I WAS CENTER. I HAD ALL YOU BASTARDS ON THE DANGLE. YOU ASK WHY I NEVER SAID ANYTHING. I SAY, WHAT ABOUT YOU?! I'D STILL BE WET FROM ONE OF THEM. I COULD SMELL MY SMELL. I'D SMILE, SAY TO MYSELF, "TODAY HE'LL SMELL MY SMELL AND FINALLY SAY IT." BUT, NO, NOT

YOU. I LEFT MY DIARY OUT. MY SUCK AND FUCK CHART I'D USE TO MARK A BOOK WE WERE BOTH READING, I'D ... I'D ... (*MARLENE cannot continue. Takes deep breath and goes back to middle of speech.*) I SAY, WHAT ABOUT YOU? I'D STILL BE WET FROM ONE OF THEM. I COULD SMELL MY SMELL. I'D SMILE, SAY ... SAY TO MYSELF, "TODAY HE'LL SMELL ... SMELL." (*MARLENE cannot continue. Let's out a muffled cry from somewhere deep. Holds stomach. Crosses to bench. Sits.*)

(*JEREMY sits. LONG SILENCE.*)

MARLENE. Doing this eight times a week's going to be a lotta fun.
JEREMY. Wait till you read the final scene!

(*BOTH laugh, JEREMY takes Marlene's hand.*)

MARLENE. Jeremy, you really ... really ...
JEREMY. Oh, Marlene!
MARLENE. Dear Jeremy!

(*JEREMY embraces Marlene, a mad, hot kiss.*)

MARLENE. Please, not the tongue right away!

(*JEREMY again with a mad, hot kiss.*)

MARLENE. (*MARLENE instantly responds. Suddenly flailing arms and moans, etc.*) What if someone sees us?
JEREMY. It's only a rewrite. (*THEY resume.*)

BLACKOUT

ACT II

Scene 3

Again, the park bench in Riverside Park in the West 80's. A month later. Morning. Just after dawn.

LIGHTS up! A long JEREMY sits on bench waiting. HE wears a black tuxedo from the evening just ended. (It was "opening night.") Bow tie loosened, tuxedo shirt hanging out. Checks watch, jumps up, moves about rubbing hands for warmth. Suddenly struck by idea, HE moves to center of bench and looks out as if at filled theatre. Holding imaginary Tony Award in hand, HE addresses imaginary audience ...

JEREMY. Thank you ladies and gentlemen and Tony voters. Thank you very much. This award I hold in my hand I totally and completely deserve. Not that the competition was in any way lacking but that I was in every way outstanding. Oh, I almost forgot! Chekhov told me just before I left that he wanted to be here but couldn't because he's hard at work on a new play called EXPLAINING THINGS TO JEREMY.

(Suddenly MARLENE appears in evening gown and mink coat with a newspaper in HER hand. However, JEREMY is so involved SHE stops, stands statue-still and listens)

JEREMY. All joking aside, I'd like to address all you future winners with the words, "FORGET YOUR GLANDS. LISTEN TO YOUR HEART. DIG DOWN AS DEEP AS THE WELL GOES. MOST OF ALL, LISTEN

TO EVERYTHING CHEKHOV TELLS YOU. LOOK, IT WORKS!!!"

(MARLENE suddenly screams, yells, claps, jumps, etc.)

JEREMY. Did you?
MARLENE. Nope.
JEREMY. Not even a quick one?
MARLENE. We agreed to here. Together. Not till now.

(MARLENE opens newspaper searching for page on which review appears. JEREMY so excited breathing is hard. Slaps chest.)

JEREMY. If it's good, you're back on top and I'm part of history.

(MARLENE laughs)

JEREMY. You wouldn't laugh if you hadn't already—
MARLENE. (*Finding page.*) JEREMY!
JEREMY. O.K., 1... 2... 3... READ!! (*JEREMY races to bench, sits. Covers ears, closes eyes, begins slow breathing.*)

(MARLENE reads, quickly let's out yelp of joy. JEREMY leaps up from bench.)

JEREMY. Are we?
MARLENE. Yup!
JEREMY. How big?!
MARLENE. Enormous!!
JEREMY. Let me read!
MARLENE. (*Reading from newspaper.*) GOD, WHAT A TOWERING TALENT FROM THE —

JEREMY. I know I'm fairly tall but —
MARLENE. My acting!
JEREMY. Oh?
MARLENE. "GOD, WHAT A TOWERING TALENT! FROM THE TIME THE CURTAIN RISES ON MS. DUMLER IN A GREENWICH VILLAGE CAFE WAITING UP UNTIL HER INCREDIBLE BREAKDOWN SPEECH WHEN SHE REVEALS KNOWING MUCH MORE THAN WE EVER EXPECTED, MS. D—
JEREMY. That's not what I intended! Why can't these bastards ever get what we intend?!
MARLENE. The last line, listen!! (*Quoting from newspaper.*) "IF YOU MISS HER, I'LL BE SURE TO MISS YOU."
JEREMY. Now read from the top!
MARLENE. (*Reading.*) "JEREMY MELVIN IS THE LUCKIEST PLAYWRIGHT IN RECENT MEMORY. HAVING CREATED A ... A TOUCHING PICTURE OF...
JEREMY. (*Grabbing paper, reading.*) "HAVING CREATED AN ENTERTAINING THOUGH SLIGHT, PROVOCATIVE YET PREDICTABLE PICTURE OF LOVE, LOSS, HATE, AND HORROR BETWEEN A DEEP WOMAN AND A SHALLOW MAN, MR. MELVIN THEN SITS BACK AND LETS THE INCREDIBLY LOVELY, SOFT, AND MULTI-TALENTED MS. DUMLER FILL IN THE MISSING GAPS AND BLATANTLY SHODDY SKIPS IN LOGIC." (*JEREMY crunches up paper.*)
MARLENE. It's a money notice. We're a huge hit!!

(*JEREMY tears paper in half.*)

MARLENE. All the T.V. were super raves! You did much better on T.V. than Chekhov did with me in *Three Sisters!*

(JEREMY tears paper several more times.)

MARLENE. *THE DAILY NEWS* says you're the discovery of the season!

(JEREMY spits at paper, punches it several times.)

MARLENE. *THE POST* calls you the funniest writer since Simon turned serious!

(JEREMY hurls paper on ground and jumps on it several times. Next HE opens fly, his intention to get it out.)

JEREMY. Erase me from history? Steal my TONY? I piss on your arrogance, *NEW YORK TIMES*.

(About to take it out but MARLENE grabs him and pulls him back. HE grabs stomach, screams, again tries to unzip, again MARLENE stops him.)

JEREMY. I am not "ENTERTAINING YET SLIGHT."
MARLENE. You're serious, you're heavy!
JEREMY. I am not "PROVOCATIVE BUT PREDICTABLE."
MARLENE. You're direct, you're a surprise a second.
JEREMY. Call me shallow? Shallow?! Shallow!!!

(Again JEREMY tries to unzip, again MARLENE stops him.)

JEREMY. Drink some of this.

MARLENE. Jeremy, you're not shallow.
JEREMY. Again.
MARLENE. You're not shallow.
JEREMY. Again.
MARLENE. You are not shallow.
JEREMY. Say, "Jeremy you're one of our last hopes!"
MARLENE. Jeremy, you're one of our last hopes.
JEREMY. Say, "You're a legend in the making!"
MARLENE. You're a legend in the making.
JEREMY. Say, "You're bleeding but you'll be back."
MARLENE. You're bleeding but you'll be back.
JEREMY. Hear that, arrogant prick!! (*Suddenly "giving finger" to newspaper on ground.*) Rotate your vegetables on this! You don't like my play? Meet me at the bank on Monday. (*Continuing to "give finger."*) Fag wimp! Putdown!! Limp Joint!!! (*Running around newspaper like a boxer over a fallen foe.*) I don't need you! You need me!! (*Suddenly a mad laugh.*) Did I tell them off or WHAT?!!

MARLENE. Wow !
JEREMY. Talk about a sustained finger job!!
MARLENE. Wow!
JEREMY. Talk about getting it all out!!!
MARLENE. Wow! (*Suddenly JEREMY puts hands in face. MARLENE sits him back and begins to rub his stomach.*)
JEREMY. Please I never let anyone.

(*MARLENE continues. JEREMY struggles but finally gives in. Like a door down deep finally opened, tears flow. HE sobs loudly. MARLENE hands him handkerchief. HE dries eyes, blows nose. HE hands her handkerchief back. SHE puts her arm around him.*)

JEREMY. I wanted so bad to be a New York big deal. So bad I wanted to tell Chekhov, "ANTON, *THE TIMES* SAYS YES." (*Silence.*) So?

MARLENE. So!

JEREMY. When do we tell him?

MARLENE. Who?

JEREMY. Herbert.

MARLENE. What about?

JEREMY. Us.

MARLENE. On the kitchen wall next to the phone hangs this thing we all call CORKBOARD OF SECRET FEELINGS AND UNSHARED ACTS. It is divided into four squares. The North West quadrant is for unshared acts. There's also along the edge three rows of colored push-pins stuck in. Yellow is for "considering it." Blue is for "soon." Red is for "already doing it." This morning it read JEREMY with four reds surrounding you.

JEREMY. Are you saying Herbert's known all along?

MARLENE. He encouraged it.

JEREMY. WHAT?!!

MARLENE. You were struggling so hard with that final scene we just ...

JEREMY. But —

MARLENE. That afternoon you went for my throat in Shubert Alley, he whispered later to me at SARDI'S, "IT'S SEXUAL. IF THAT'S WHAT IT TAKES, DO IT!"

JEREMY. But ... But ... what about in the boiler room after the first run-through?

MARLENE. Talk about multiples!

JEREMY. What about at The Mayflower?

MARLENE. The best ever!!

JEREMY. I was so sure you and I— (*Suddenly stops.*) Were you even for a second ever?

MARLENE. Ever what?

JEREMY. Tempted?

MARLENE. Yes.

JEREMY. How often?

MARLENE. For one whole afternoon of rehearsal I entertained the thought of getting back!

JEREMY. What stopped you?

MARLENE. You can write about it but you can't live it every day. Me, all I live for is acting. Buddy, we're two half people who together don't add up to one.

JEREMY. O God! (*Suddenly taking note pad from pocket, JEREMY scribbles madly.*)

MARLENE. What's wrong?

JEREMY. I just figured out the first act ending to my new play.

MARLENE. How many characters?

JEREMY. Two.

MARLENE. Man and a woman?

JEREMY. Two men.

MARLENE. What's it called?

JEREMY. *Talking Things Over With My Old Chick's New Old Man.*

MARLENE. You devil! Herbert'll be so proud!!

JEREMY. This new one's a whole two levels deeper than the one you're doing now.

MARLENE. What about tonight?!

JEREMY. I don't follow.

MARLENE. We're having some people over tonight for drinks and dinner. Many of them backers. All of them fans. They'd love to hear you read it. O God, I knew we could all be friends. Finally, you and Herbert get to sit down and really—

JEREMY. I'll be 3,000 miles away.

MARLENE. LA?

JEREMY. Chekhov and I are on the United noon flight.

MARLENE. Movie offer for our play?

JEREMY. Yup.

MARLENE. Which studio?

JEREMY. Bad luck till it's locked in.

MARLENE. I'll be rooting for you.

JEREMY. I'll push for you but then again it is the movies.

MARLENE. The original Broadway cast almost always gets dumped.

JEREMY. Everything's worked out so far. (*Suddenly pointing toward Hudson River.*) Look.

MARLENE. Where?

JEREMY. It's him.

MARLENE. Who?

JEREMY. Over by the railing in the white suit. I'm not exactly sure I—

JEREMY. He's waving. (*JEREMY waves.*) Wave back.

MARLENE. (*Waves.*) He's holding up a white cardboard sign.

JEREMY. That's all he does anymore. Magic marker on his white signs.

MARLENE. O God! It's to me!! (*Reads aloud.*) "MARLENE, YOU ELEVATE HIS WORK. LAST NIGHT YOU WERE INSPIRED."

JEREMY. Look, another sign.

MARLENE. "I ALSO LOVED YOU FIVE YEARS AGO IN *THREE SISTERS* YOU'RE MY BEST MASHA SINCE OLGA K.

JEREMY. Olga K. means Olga Knipper.

MARLENE. Look, for you!

JEREMY. (*Reading aloud.*) "JEREMY, NO WISE-GUY STUFF. KEEP YOUR TONGUE TO YOURSELF. SAY GOOD-BY NICE." (*JEREMY opens arms, hugs MARLENE warmly.*) See you in a week or so.

MARLENE. Take care.

JEREMY. Gotta run.

MARLENE. Hurry back. I'll need a new play for next season.

(JEREMY rushes off, MARLENE waves "goodby." MARLENE sits on bench, about to be sad—as JEREMY bursts back on in a winded rush.)

MARLENE. What's wrong?
JEREMY. He wants to photograph us together.

(THEY sit together on bench. Quickly find comfortable position holding each other's hands. For a very long time nothing happens.)

MARLENE. What's taking him so long?
JEREMY. He's never used a flash before.

(Suddenly two FLASHES go off. BOTH leap to feet only MARLENE suddenly points toward Chekhov.)

MARLENE. Look, another message.
JEREMY. "I WANT TO SHOOT A WHOLE ROLL. PLEASE STAY STILL AND JUST SMILE."

(THEY sit back on bench, take original positions, hand in hand.)

MARLENE. How's that?
JEREMY. How's this?

(BOTH assume posed smiles. As LIGHTS begin to fade to dark, flashbulb FLASHES fill the descending light.)

COSTUME PLOT

I-1
JEREMY: Sweat suit (mismatched, old); old sneakers; ratty sweat cap

MARLENE: Sweat suit (stylish and new); new running shoes; oversized sunglasses, new cap

I-2
JEREMY: Ratty hat, ratty coat, same sneakers, ratty gloves
MARLENE: Beautiful wool suit, jewelry, high heels, alligator pocketbook

I-3
JEREMY: Bowler hat, walking cane, three-piece suit, same sneakers
MARLENE: Old sweater, old skirt, old shoes

II-1
JEREMY: Same suit as in I-3
MARLENE: Sexy red dress, high heels, jewelry

II-2
JEREMY: Oversized coat, bandage on one eye, same sneakers
MARLENE: Same running outfit as in I-1.

II-3
MARLENE: Fur, gown, high heels, jewelry
JEREMY: Tuxedo, same sneakers as usual

PROPERTY PLOT

Six copies of play in binders (Jeremy)
Pen, pad (Marlene)
One dozen red roses (Jeremy)
Six copies of play in binders, notes on revisions (Marlene)
Copy of *New York Times* (Marlene)
Camera with flash (Chekhov)

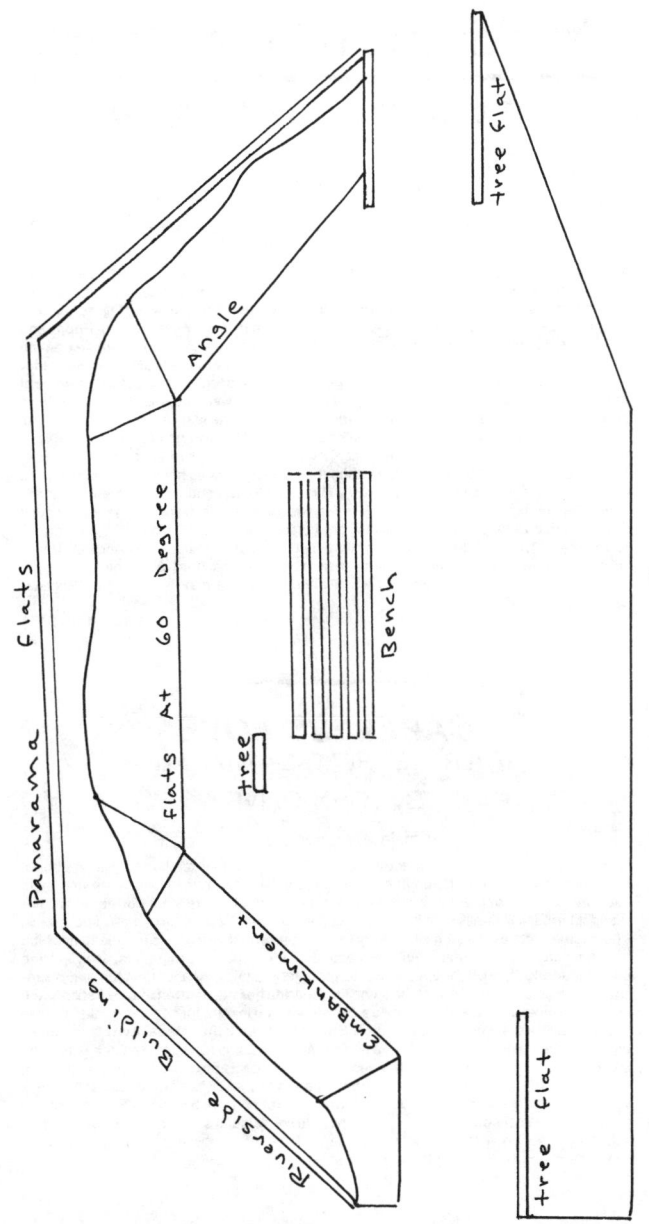

Other Publications for Your Interest

THE VOICE OF THE PRAIRIE
(LITTLE THEATRE—COMIC/DRAMA)
By JOHN OLIVE

2 men, 1 women—to play a variety of roles
May be done with up to 10 actors—Unit Setting

When this play begins, we are listening to an old hobo (named "Poppy" by his avid companion young Davey Quinn) tell a tall tale. It is the early 1890's, and itinerant story tellers such as Poppy really were the voices of the prairie. Many years later, when Davey is grown up, he is "discovered" by radio entrepreneur Leon Schwab, telling his tales of Poppy and of Frankie the Blind Girl, whom he rescued from a cruel father and with whom he went on a cross-country adventure. Schwab thinks Quinn's stories would attract an audience for radio, the "wave of the future". Sure enough, David Quinn becomes famous as the Voice of the Prairie, as the cleverly-constructed play cross-cuts between scenes of Leon and David and scenes of young Davey and Frankie the Blind Girl, on the lam, in search of adventure. These scenes culminate in the unfortunate separation of Davey and Frankie, as Frankie is recognized, captured and sent back home. David Quinn, the grown-up Voice of the Prairie, has not seen or heard from her since; until, that is, Leon locates her in hopes of using his discovery of the actual, famous Frankie the Blind Girl for its sentimental value, to keep the new F.C.C. off his back. Will David forgive Frankie for leaving him so many years ago? Will Frankie agree to help Leon avoid jail for broadcasting without a license? "Endearing."—N.Y. Times. "That rare thing: a small, skillful play with a deft heart."—Los Angeles Times. "Beguiling entertainment and as American as corn."—Hartford Advocate. "First-rate entertainment. I can't remember when I last so enjoyed a play."—Torrington Register Citizen. Slightly Restricted.

(#24047)

CARELESS LOVE
(LITTLE THEATRE—DRAMA)
By JOHN OLIVE

1 male, 1 woman—Unit set

What a terrific little play for an actress and actor to sink their teeth into! And, it's about something that matters: commitment, and responsibility, in love. When we first meet Jack, he is an aspiring actor, serious about his career but not very serious about his girlfriend, Martha, a waitress who is an aspiring dancer, who is a lot more serious about Jack. The couple drifts along on a cloud of good times — until Martha gets pregnant, at which time a *Choice* must be made. As the debate over their options progresses, Jack's acting career starts to take off; and, he starts to think more seriously about his life and his responsibilities. Unfortunately, at the same time Martha has been driven into self-absorption by Jack's carelessness, and has made a decision which is right for her, she thinks: she has decided to give the child up for adoption. So — at just about the time Jack is ready to make an emotional commitment to Martha and to their child, it is too late: Martha has had the baby and put it up for adoption. This was, after all, *her* decision to make. Right? In the end, Martha is a self-sufficient contemporary woman, who makes her own choices. It is Jack who will hurt forever, from the pain of eternal separation from his child. "Bittersweet." — Variety. "In the delicacy of its writing, in the truth of its details...it is a most lovely, most satisfying evening in the theatre."—Chicago Tribune. "A lovely little play...works a winsome magic."—Philadelphia Daily News.

(#5237)

Other Publications for Your Interest

LLOYD'S PRAYER
(LITTLE THEATRE—COMEDY)

By KEVIN KLING

3 men, 1 woman (1 man & 1 woman play various parts). Bare stage w/set pieces.

Be amazed! The author of the amazing *21A* has fashioned a hilarious comic parable about Bob, the Raccoon Boy, and what happens to him when he is "rescued" from the raccoons who raised him and taught what it means to be human. At first, Bob can only make whirring raccoon sounds, but he is taught to speak by a delightfully whacko "Mom and Dad". He is taken from his cage at Mom and Dad's house by an ambitious ex-con named Lloyd, who sees the raccoon boy as his ticket to fame and fortune. When his first idea—displaying Bob as a carny sideshow freak—fails, Lloyd gets the brilliant idea to become a religious evangelist, displaying Bob as another sort of freak: a miracle from God. Lloyd's pitch, a promise of inspiration "that will bring grown men to a sitting position and women to a greater understanding of themselves", makes them both celebrities. By this time, Bob speaks pretty well ("I've been called many things in my life...But I prefer 'Bob'"), and is on the verge of innocence corrupted when there appears on the scene a beautiful guardian angel, dressed as a high school cheerleader. "Be amazed!", she declares, admonishing Bob to beware of Lloyd. What ensues is an amusing tug-of-war between the angel and Lloyd, with Bob the Raccoon Boy as the rope. The unqualified hit of the Actors Theatre of Louisville 1988 Humana Festival, this brilliant new comedy is "a whirlwind of original humor that comes in waves."—Lexington Herald-Leader. "Fresh, funny and charming."—Columbus Dispatch. "Kling is quite simply a comic genius."—Dramatics Magazine.

(#13997)

21A
(ADVANCED GROUPS—COMEDY)

By KEVIN KLING

1 man—Bare stage w/chairs.

"Astonishing", was the way Newsweek Magazine summed up this one-man tour-de-force in which Mr. Kling performed all the riders on a Minneapolis city bus: eight characters, including the driver. Structured as a series of monologues which in "real life" are going on simultaneously, this hilarious and decidedly "different" play had them rolling in the aisles at Louisville's famed Humana Festival where it won the prestigious Heideman Award. Kling started with the droll driver and moved on to such odd-balls as Gladys, Chairman Francis (a religious proselytizer), Captain Twelve-Pack (a drunk with a beer 12-pack box over his head) and a businessman who is decidedly *not* "Dave", no matter how fervently Captain Twelve-Pack insists that he *is*. And: who is the mysterious intruder sitting at the back of the bus? "Stunning."—U.S.A. Today.

(#22237)

Other Publications for Your Interest

ALONE AT THE BEACH
(LITTLE THEATRE—COMEDY)
By RICHARD DRESSER

4 men, 3 women—Combination Interior/Exterior

"So you thought the kind of comedy that sends audiences home happy had disappeared from the American theatre scene? *"Wrong!"* enthused the Louisville Courier-Journal over this literate, witty comedy, which had the audience at Actors Theatre of Louisville's famed Humana Festival whooping with laughter. George, a mild-mannered man in his mid-30's, has inherited a beach house in the Hamptons on Long Island. In order to afford to keep it, he has let out rooms to boarders, Manhattan-ites desparate to get out of the city on weekends. Blindly, and blithely, George has not actually *met* any of these denizens of the yuppie sector of the urban jungle. If everyone were Great Fun and Easy To Get Along With, everyone would have a great time—but the audience, of course, wouldn't. Who wants to watch a bunch of friendly, well-adjusted people have Fun In The Sun? Thankfully, Dresser gives us a motley crew of urban neurotics, male and female, who begin to drive George, and everyone else, crazy the moment they arrive. Somehow, though, everyone survives the experience, egos intact; and, in fact, some of the most unlikely romances develop, before everyone has to face reality: Labor Day and, subsequently, the trek back to New York City for good—until next summer? "Has a unique sparkle." New Albany Tribune. "A winner...a riotously funny sex farce."—Detroit News. "A charming romp that should turn up in regional and community theatres all over the place."—Houston Post. "Has the pacing of a Neil Simon script but with some of the dry, more cerebral wit of Jules Feiffer."—Evansville Courier.

(#3118)

EMILY
(ADVANCED GROUPS—SERIOUS COMEDY)
By STEPHEN METCALFE

8 men, 4 women, to play a variety of roles.
Bare stage, w/drops, wings, projections & wagons; or, may be unit set.

This brilliant, cynical, contemporary new comedy by the author of *Strange Snow, Vikings, Sorrows and Sons* and *The Incredibly Famous Willy Rivers* dares to take what amounts to a politically "incorrect" stance about the successful "New Woman." Emily is a successful New York City stockbroker who mixes it up with the boys and always comes out on top. In fact, she was described by one misguided critic as coming off like a "man in drag"; because, as we all know, women are caring, loving, nurturing creatures—and what a wonderful world it would be if *they* were in positions of political and/or business power, instead of those insensitive jerks, the *men*. Emily is just as cynical and ruthless as any man in her position; until, that is, she meets a caring, sensitive, aspiring actor (in other words, a nice guy with no money) who doesn't fall for her manipulative ruses; but, rather, for the real Emily he sees inside the ruthless yuppie—who may, or may not, exist. "Glorious...a sparkling comedy with bite to it. The title character is a gold mine of a role for an actress."—San Diego Tribune. "A real winner...a bravura balancing act right on the edge of sentimentality, finally and triumphantly crystalline in its emotional honesty...A triumph." —San Diego Union.

(#7076)